Fast Women Beautiful

ACKNOWLEDGEMENTS

Thanks to the editors and publishers of the following publications where some of these poems first appeared: *Ant Farm, Bottom Line, Bulldog Breath, Jack Magazine, The Kerouac Connection, Memo, Pen & Sword, The Redwood Coast Review, Stone's Throw,* and *Zam Bomba!* Thanks to Zoe Artemis for coining the phrase "zen beat baseball poems."

A Tenacity Press Book

Tenacity Press, founded by Hal Zina Bennett and Susan J. Sparrow in 1992, follows the tenets of a literary cooperative. We join an honored tradition of small publishers who through the centuries have championed the works of fine authors. For more information: www. TenacityPress.org

Fast Women Beautiful

Zen Beat Baseball Poems

Daniel Barth

To Linda
in Ukiah
at Mendocino Litfest
5/2/09

Happy Derby Day!

Daniel Barth

TENACITY PRESS

iUniverse, Inc.
New York Bloomington Shanghai

Fast Women Beautiful
Zen Beat Baseball Poems

Copyright © 2008 by Daniel J. Barth

iUniverse books may be ordered through booksellers or by contacting:

iUniverse
1663 Liberty Drive
Bloomington, IN 47403
www.iuniverse.com
1-800-Authors (1-800-288-4677)

ISBN: 978-0-595-49652-5 (pbk)
ISBN: 978-0-595-61194-2 (ebk)

Printed in the United States of America

Contents

Introduction

In one of his talks on writing, Billy Collins said the theme of all great poetry is *carpe diem*, that is, "seize the day." I don't know if that's always true, and Billy probably doesn't either. But I do know that one of the first things that drew me to Dan Barth's poetry was the immediacy of his work, that is, how his imagery and subject matter pulled my focus into everyday life, made me pay attention to the elusive present. Very *carpe diemish*! Whether he is telling us about driving a delivery truck in Louisville, Kentucky, for the Coca-Cola Bottling Company, or describing a Zen master sitting in the sun doing a crossword puzzle, Dan knows what it takes to remind us to seize the day.

I love it when poetry does this.

I understand it's smart in an essay of this kind to trace the poet's influences, to compare his imagery, his cadence and line, to the great poets before him. But I've always considered that academic posturing, and even considering doing that with Dan's work seems inappropriate at best. Not inappropriate because he doesn't deserve to be taken seriously in that way but inappropriate because he deserves *not* to be taken seriously in that way. However, there is an appropriate way to take him seriously, and we should.

The influences that show through most strongly in his writing are things like *fast women, beautiful horses, banjos, bluegrass, and bourbon*—lines picked out of his title poem, if you must know.

I remember four of us sitting around a greasy table at a truck stop in northern California one evening, eating hamburgers and French fries as our conversation glided smoothly through hitchhiking, Buddhism, getting drunk, Ferlinghetti, jail, beautiful women, and baseball, as if they were all just yarns in some intriguing tapestry that had woven its way in Dan's mind. And so it is with this wonderful collection of his poems. It's a lot like that evening at the truck stop, sin burgers and fries. He means what the subtitle of his book says; these really are Zen, Beat, baseball poems.

There's a sometimes brooding under layer in Dan's poetry that is, at one and the same time, as American as ... well, baseball ... and as anti-American as Kerouac or Ginsberg. It's troubling because it implies that we should keep our priorities straight about not losing sight of what matters in life. Seize the day.

But then I promised not to get all academic-like and trace the poet's influences. When you really get what's Dan's writing is about—listen to his "pomes," as he calls them, in your head—you learn that for him those guys like Whitman, Snyder, Ferlinghetti, Kesey, and Corso didn't so much influence him as they are just part of the music that runs through his brain, blending together with Rock 'n Roll, Blues, Bluegrass and cats coming in from the rain.

And you know, when he says as he does in some poem or other in this book, that he sits on the front porch, pen and notebook ready, waiting to sing another mad song, he really means it because that's what poetry is about for him.

Further proof of what Billy says.

Carpe diem. Damn right!

—Hal Zina Bennett

Hal Zina Bennett is the author of *The Lens of Perception, Write from the Heart* and numerous other books.

The Old Runner

the old distance runner
eases out

settles into his pace

hears the creek flow
feels the wind blow
sees the sun shine
knows his right mind

he's old and slow
but he can still go

he stretches before and after

he drinks a lot of water

Zen Pome

Zen Master in the afternoon
sits down to his crossword puzzle and tea

the first sip is insouciance
one down is clams

the second sip is enlightenment
one across is came

the third sip is compassion
23 across is same

*

the simple humble beauty of life
the grokking insouciance of trees
standing still like the hummingbird
he sees

*

Zen Master in the afternoon
sits down to his mushrooms and tea

Zen Master at night
has fun with his Roshi rum

Buddha Pome

buddha buddha
who is this buddha?
he is buddha beer drinker
buddha who is kind
buddha before the fire
buddha who sits calmly with cats
he is buddha latte drinker
buddha who masturbates, oh baby
buddha who gets upset
buddha in the woodpile
buddha watch the river flow
buddha watch the watch
he is buddha bunny rabbit
chicken buddha
buddha ba dump bump tells bad jokes
buddha walks up to a hot dog vendor
says: make me one with everything
buddha who cooks breakfast lunch dinner
buddha duz the dishes
he is buddha blue sky
buddha white cloud
buddha who rakes leaves
buddha leaves being raked
buddha who plays basketball
buddha net
buddha empty hoop
he is buddha basketball coach
brooding buddha
ping-pong buddha
tennis elbow buddha
lower back pain buddha
exercycle buddha
treadmill buddha
buddha teacher late for class
buddha poetry scribbler

buddha story teller
buddha librarian
buddha mosquito swatter
buddha who drives old bus
buddha bike rider

buddha who walks
he is health club buddha
hot tub buddha
sauna sweat buddha

buddha who stretches
he is feet up easy chair lazy buddha
tv control flip the channels buddha
buddha baseball fan
      if zen is poetry
      and poetry is zen
      and baseball is poetry
      then baseball is zen
      Q. E. D.
he is i. e., e. g., Q. E. D. buddha
grammar, syntax, usage buddha
buddha of big loud farts

moody buddha
nobody buddha
everyday ordinary buddha
buddha kind to frogs
buddha bird feeder
      fuck peacocks
      he likes titmice, towhees and ducks
kittycat buddha with mind of tall clover
chainsaw buddha
branchlopper buddha
walk in the rain watch the creek flow buddha
alone with book under lamp

does a dog have the buddha nature?
grrrfff!

if you meet this buddha on the road
say howdy

What Is the Secret
of Vishnu's Maya?

They say it's all the play
of opposites; it's all done
with mirrors, or
maybe it's just a dream
that people live,
that people die:
they say in the end
it's the blink of an eye.

I Used to Drive

1.

My dad was personnel manager
for the Coca-Cola Bottling Co.
on Hill Street
in Louisville
in the 1960s
and '70s.
My brother
and cousins
and friends
and I
got summer
and Christmastime
jobs there in those days.
I worked five summers
and at least four
Christmases.
Summers were hot and humid.
Winters were cold and bleak.
It was not easy work.
But I earned enough money
to help pay my way
at college.
And I gotta admit
I learned a lot
about Louisville
and people
and the workaday world.

2.

I used to drive
Coke trucks
on days like this—
hot, muggy,
summer days in Kentucky.
I would drive to
country clubs
with swimming pools
where beautiful girls
lay around in bikinis
and middle-aged matrons
slurped drinks, played bridge,
played tennis (the thinner,
more athletic ones).
I used to drive River Road,
Bardstown Road,
Taylorsville Road,
Beulah Church Road,
Westport Road,
LaGrange Road,
and even
Mockingbird Valley Road
on hot
muggy
summer
days
like
this.

3.

I used to drive Coke trucks
to racetracks
in Louisville
in the old days
in Kentucky
when I was a kid.
I drove to Miles Park,
Louisville Downs,
Churchill Downs
and carried 30-pound tanks
of coke, sprite, orange, tab
to track kitchens,
jockeys' quarters,
bars and
concession stands.
Arriving early,
glancing at yesterday's losers'
tossed away tickets,
I'd do my job
and leave.
But yes,
sometimes I did linger
on the bricks
in the shade
at Churchill Downs
and look up
at the names
of Derby winners
and muse
and wonder,
plan
and dream.

4.

I used to drive Coke trucks
to bars in Louisville.
I started my route
at 8 AM.
They had been open since 6:00.
In the dim light
old men
read newspapers,
Racing Forms;
drank coffee,
beer, bourbon,
muscatel over ice.
Top o' the mornin'.
One old owner
on Preston Street
always paid me in ones.
Usually it was 32 dollars.
He'd count out each one
slowly into my palm.
Then back in the truck—
1st gear, 2nd gear,
3rd gear, 4th gear—
through traffic
to the next bar,
dim light,
old men,
morning drink,
Racing Form
life.

5.

At Coke Station
on Preston Highway
they served a hot lunch.
Home cooking.
Cafeteria style.

Overweight ladies served
one meat, two vegetables,
bread & butter, iced tea,
for $2.95.
Workingmen washed their hands,
went through the line.
What'll it be?
I'll have the chicken.
How 'bout you?
I'll try the chops.
Give me the green beans.
Noodles. Potatoes.
Cole slaw. Thank you.
Thank you ma'am.
You're welcome.

Choose a table.
Sit down.
Tired.
Hungry.
Time to eat.
Shoot the shit.
A half-hour of sad
happiness, then
back to work.

6.

I used to drive Coke trucks
to Lions Clubs, Elks Lodges,
Eagles Eyries
all around the greater
Indiucky area.
Turners Park. Swiss Park.
The All Wool and Yard Wide Democratic Club.
In afternoon clubhouse bars
old men watched ballgames,
gossiped, played cards,
smoked Camels, Pall Malls,
Winstons, Raleighs;
drank Falls City Beer,
Sterling Beer, Oertle's '92.
"Son, I tellya, I used to
drink that Falls City Beer
and eat those White Castle hamburgers.
Got so I couldn't shit a hard turd."
At the Redmen's Club
in Jeffersonville
they had a slot machine.
Illegal, yes,
but the local constable
was a member.
The Elks in Lyndon
had a baseball field.
"We just like to feel like
we're doin' somethin' for the kids."
The Masons
in St. Matthews
ran an orphanage.
Widows and orphans.
Annual picnic.
Thirty-three degrees of initiation.

"Hey, here's the Coke man.
Glad ta see ya, son.
We're outa that Sprite
and old Elmer here
has been complainin'."

7.

Old men used to tell me things.

One guy told me how he
literally fucked the shit
out of his old lady—
"Oh, I was goin' at 'er
and bangin' 'er and bangin' 'er
good and hard.
And when we finished
she rolled over
and there was a little turd
lyin' right there on the bed sheet."

One old guy lamented—
"Ah, when I was young
I'd be so hard
in the morning
I could stand and
pee backwards
over my head.
Now I'm lucky
if I don't dribble on my toes."

And one guy told me—
"My old lady
ain't never had much problem
with headaches.
But yeast infections?!?
Shit!!!
I ain't never seen nothin'
so many things can go wrong with
as a pussy."

8.

You think there weren't problems?
You think people weren't
racist
and sexist
in Louisville
in the '60s?
Think again.
"Shit, there goes a nigger
with a white girl,"
another driver told me,
"seein' somethin' like that
ruins my whole day."
—"Yah, that's women's work."
—"Yah, that's a nigger job."
—"Yah, he's a faggot.
—"Shit, look at that nigger
drivin' a Cadillac.
Must be a pimp.
Probly on welfare.
Shit."

You think people
weren't racist
and sexist
in Louisville
in the 1960s
and '70s?
You think people
aren't still?
Think
again.

Win Some, Lose Some

That night I spent the night in jail I left Gerstle's place
1 A. M. to hitchhike to my sister's and watch U of L play
basketball on tv, the Great Alaska Shootout. I was
carrying one of those oil-can-sized 22 ounce Foster's Lagers.
I had already opened it. I was walking and hitching
when the cop pulled over—Officer Diggs, Figgs, something
like that. "Pour out that beer," was the first thing he said.
"Oh, man, I just opened it." "Pour it out." "Okay." "You know
it's against the law to hitchhike," he said. I couldn't believe
it, didn't think, just blurted out, "It's not against the law to
hitchhike." That was all it took. He threw me up against the
car, slapped on the cuffs, shoved me into the backseat. I
complained, pleaded and wheedled all the way downtown.
Under the courthouse I was booked, fingerprinted,
photographed. "What'd you do, piss off a cop?"
the friendly fingerprint man asked me.
"Yeah, I guess." Next it was holding cell
with all the other Friday night drunks.
I used my one phone call to call my sister
but no one there could offer any help.
"Hang in there," they told me.
Then to the regular all-night drunk tank
but not before we had to strip and spread our cheeks.
"I don't play that," one old dude informed the guard,
who responded, "You want a piece of me?"
"Shit, buncha faggots," the old dude grumbled,
but he spread, we all did. In the drunk tank
everybody flopped out. I couldn't sleep. Oh, but
first they issued cigarettes all around. What a nightmare! I've
never been a smoker. One guy fell asleep with a Camel burning
between his fingers. It burned almost all the way down. I
grabbed it away, thinking to keep him from getting burned.
That woke him up. "Smoke your own," he growled. 6 A. M.
I was released. "Don't let me see you here again," warned
the guard. "I don't intend to." "Arraignment's at eight." "Okay."

I walked the cold downtown Louisville streets till then, made my appearance, got a court date set, and limped on home.

In Anchorage, Alaska, U of L lost to N. C. State, 72-66. The next year they won their first National Championship.

Fast Women Beautiful

Fast women beautiful horses
banjos bluegrass bourbon
it's a region it's a religion it's a
way of life and on the first
Saturday in May it all comes
together for two heart-pounding
minutes at Churchill Downs race-
track in Louisville someday you
gotta go there sometime you
gotta see it by god it's wonderful
it's amazing there's nothing else
like it it's the Kentucky Derby

Go For Gin

His foddah was a muddah,
His muddah was a muddah,
And he was a muddah too.
He won the Derby going away,
Against a field of 13 other
Highly rated three-year-olds,
On a sloppy track,
On a very rainy day,
Churchill Downs racetrack,
Louisville, Kentucky,
May 7, 1994,
First Saturday in May.

Monohan-an
after Snyder

In memorium, the Old Monohan Place, last farm in the East
End/Breckinridge Road area of Louisville. Still alive in 1980, with
fish in stream, herons nesting. Now, like all the rest, gone under for
houses, roads, restaurants, mini-marts and strip malls.

sun breaks over wind-
break below corn field
Mary's having tea
I sit at the table
and write

distant dogs bark, a pair of
cooing doves; the toweet
of a cardinal high in a pine
behind the bedroom window
Mar lies back in bed, lazing

a soft continuous roar
comes across the fields
of the interstate highway—
thousands and thousands of cars
driving folks to church

Photo Op

Sunday morning
Cincinnati, Ohio
McDonald's "photo spot"
flag at half mast
for pardoned criminal
former President
of these States.
Four redbirds play on lawn.
Billions and billions served.

Hawley-Cookery
in memory of Elizabeth Cooke

In a suburban sprawl of strip malls,
Gas stations, mini-marts, fast-
Food restaurants and liquor barns
We sit a bookstore.
We sit a terrific bookstore,
To invite, to entice people away
From the more mundane pleasures
Of everyday existence, we write.
And people want,
You know people want
These things. We try to give
The people what they need.

Mardi Gras

soft southern

early morning

streetcar

Edith Piaf in the rain

garbage men done
been and gone

nuther natchral
Mardi Gras
gathering momentum

natural wonders abound
geeks freak in the streets
hoofbeats heart
hoofbeats heard
hard hoofbeats in the street
natchral bacchanal
bourbon and canal
nawlans
nawlanz
naw lance

Miller's crazy
wantsa be rich
wants some
COCAINE
ain't it a bitch
old lady leavin'
middle of a party
she packed her bag
didn'even say goodbye

oh she'll be back
say she'll be

    ain't it a bitch
wish i was rich
    it's gonna kill me
i need some
      COCAINE

          heartbeats
          hoofbeats

    natchral

in the early morning light
i like to get it right—
sit down and say what i mean

on the trolley and the bus
folks discuss what's up—
it's Shrovetide in old New Orleans

That Kind of Horse

You knew what kind of a horse
He was when you bet on him—
Beautiful but uncertain—
Perfect in the paddock,
Fractious in the gate,
Gliding effortlessly along the backside,
But losing interest in the stretch.
Well, he came in second didn't he?
Why the hell do you always bet them to win?

Variation on Extemporaneous Lines by Franz Cilensek

The bald bookseller scampers
to fill my request,
a cloth bound edition
of *Lady Chatterly's Lover.*
Failing to find it, he
attempts to distract me
with meaningless computer chatter.
I tell him (kindly), I don't care
about computers, no offense,
brother, but if you don't have
D. H. Lawrence, in hardcover,
I'm out of this bookstore,
bound for another.

Ten Thousand Blessings

Books are a wonder and a blessing
Not possessed but kept in trust
You should see the Library at the Buddhist University
Come with me some afternoon and wander through the stacks
Books arranged by Ch'an logic
Emily Dickinson here and there
Hemingway high and low
Chinese folk tales one aisle, Japanese another
Norman Vincent Peale comfy with Carlos Castaneda
Picasso nudes, Modigliani foldouts
These take-the-vows bhikshus will surprise you
Come with me and you'll see too
So many wonders, ten thousand blessings

Stealing Bibles from the Buddhist School

There's a good-sized section on religion
In the Buddhist Boys School Library.
Subheadings include Judaism, Taoism, Hinduism,
Islam, Buddhism of course, and Christianity.

At one time there were a good many Bibles
On the Christianity shelf. But one by one,
Over the years, these Bibles have disappeared.
Leatherbound King James, hardcover Oxford Annotated,
Softcover Good News, somehow, without
Being checked out or accounted for,
All the Bibles but one have left the shelf.

What is going on here? How is this happening?
Is there a secret cadre of Christians among the Buddhists?
Are bhikshus and bhikshunis meeting clandestinely
To chant sutras and speak in tongues?
Is there some hybrid religion in the offing?
Buddheo Christianity? Pentecostal Zen?
Or are the Bibles merely being censored, hidden, destroyed?
What kind of dynamic is at work I wonder.

Here's what I would like to know:
Why is someone stealing Bibles from the Buddhist school?

Three Dog Neighborhood
for Jim Hsiang

Pretty straightforward this one,
About my friend Pete and his wife Susan.
They bought an old house in Denver
Down on the Platte River.
Shortly thereafter their tv got stolen.
They bought a dog, a good-sized dog,
To kind of keep an eye on things.
But it didn't help, they were burgled again.
This time the investigating officer said:
"You live in a three dog neighborhood."
"Huh?" said Pete (not in a good mood).
"One for the front yard, one for the back yard,
One for the house," explained the cop—
"Three dog neighborhood."
"Yeah, right," said Pete, "Now I'm hip."

Throwing Dharma Gifts in the Dumpster

A chair sits in a corner
Of the Buddhist school library
All summer. In the fall,
When school starts up again,
That chair is full of books—
Dharma Gifts—
That have been donated
By well-meaning Buddhists.

The librarian's difficult decision:
Which books to keep, which to throw out.

Some of the books of course
Are quite lovely and useful.
Others are worse than worthless
For a school library, or any library.
How many *Readers Digest Condensed Books*
And back issues of *National Geographic*
Can any library afford shelf space?

Inevitably some of the Dharma Gifts
Must be discarded.

A moonlit September night
Finds the decisive librarian
Doing a necessary part of his job,
Surreptitiously—

Throwing Dharma Gifts in the dumpster.

Four Artists Out of a Dream

Utrillo, Modigliani, Van Gogh and Gauguin go out to lunch.
"I want to paint the streets of Montmartre," says Utrillo.
"I want to paint the women of France," says Modigliani.
"I want to paint everything," says Van Gogh.
"I want to go to Tahiti," says Gauguin.

Utrillo, Modigliani, Van Gogh and Gauguin relax in a cafe.
"I want to drink until I see visions," says Utrillo.
"I want to fuck until I see visions," says Modigliani.
"I see visions!" says Van Gogh.
"How much is a one way ticket to Tahiti?" says Gauguin.

Utrillo, Modigliani, Van Gogh and Gauguin sit late at table.
Utrillo passes out on the floor.
Modigliani leaves with a whore.
Van Gogh shoots a game of pool.
Gauguin writes a letter to his wife.

Utrillo, Modigliani, Van Gogh and Gauguin go their separate ways.
Utrillo paints a Montmartre street with a hangover.
Modigliani paints the woman of the previous night.
Van Gogh paints the cafe.
Gauguin walks down to the wharf.

Philosophers Club

The welcoming party of wild grains,
The wild rice gang,
Encounter their adversaries,
Take them out to lunch,
Argue fine points of theology and philosophy.
How many angels on the head of a pin?
Sound of one hand clapping?
Which came first, egg or chicken?
What's the difference between a duck?

Lunch gives way to serious sake drinking.
Reasoned argument turns to name calling.
You intentionally obfuscating, self-deluded
            Hegelian son of a bitch.
Yeah, your argument's so circular it's makin' me dizzy.
Your mama is so Kierkegaardian that only a self that
            relates itself to itself and is therefore grounded
            in a power higher than itself would want to fuck her.
Don't you be talkin' 'bout my mama!

After that, order is never restored.
Fisticuffs mix with fragments of invective:
Zen fascist bastard! Baudrillardian neo-Nazi!
Your German accent sucks!

The party of wild grains boards a houseboat for home.
Their guests curse them roundly and depart by train.
Plans for next year's meeting will be arranged by mail.

Frank Among the Poets
for Leslie and Frank Roberts

He agrees to accompany his lovely
Intelligent wife to the poetry reading,
For moral support. She is to read.
He loves her. Maybe there won't be
Too many poems about death, despair,
Suicide, blood dripping from veins.
Maybe not too many sensitive souls
Will drone on and on about their woebegone
Lives. He'll hang in there, Frank figures,
It can't be that bad, and hey, anyway,
His wife, his partner, the mother of his
Children, will be reading. He knows she's okay.
And besides, Lord help him, he loves her.

Van Gogh's Crows

Biographers say he was schizophrenic, suicidal.
Psychologists say the crows represent
All the dark forces of his psyche
Rising up to engulf him.
But maybe
There were just a lot of crows
In the field that day.

Electric Prisms, Circular Forms

Looking through a book on Abstract Painting I come upon
Sonia Delaunay * Electric Prisms, Robert Delaunay * Circular Forms
With shock of recognition. These seem to be exactly
The colors I saw in mind's eye while drifting off to sleep
Last night. How can this be? I had never read
The book before. Yes, it was near my head as I drifted
Off. The old theory? Sleep with book under
Pillow? No need to study, absorb knowledge all night?
But the colors, the colors! How did I know those
Shapes and colors? They existed. They exist. They will
Continue to exist, independent of Sonia Delaunay, Robert
Delaunay, certainly independent of me—
Electric Prisms, Circular Forms.

Hiawatha Sticky Fingers
(Listening to the Rolling Stones
while Reading Longfellow)

On a disc called Sticky Fingers
The Rolling Stones belt out "Brown Sugar"
While the noble Hiawatha
Sings his war song wild and woeful.
Wild, wild horses and war eagles
Swirl and sway and intermingle,
Scream and hurtle through the heavens.

Hiawatha sends his challenge
To the mightiest of magicians:
"Come out! Can't you hear me knockin'?
You gotta move for Hiawatha!"

Then they fight a mighty battle
And he kills the great magician.

Hiawatha falls to longing.
"It's a bitch!" says Hiawatha,
"I got the blues. I need a woman."

In the land of the Dacotahs
Sings the maiden Minnehaha:
"Tell me, tell me, Hiawatha,
When are you comin' 'round again?"

To the land of the Dacotahs
Journeys mighty Hiawatha,
Woos and wins fair Minnehaha;
Then they journey home together.

Just about a moonlight mile, the rock band,
The Rolling Stones, the greatest rock band,

Send dead flowers to the wedding,
Send dead flowers by the mail,
Leaving Hiawatha happy
With the night and Minnehaha.

The record's over, I stop reading;
Turn off the stereo, turn on the tv
To a rerun of Leave it to Beaver.
A fight between the brothers Cleaver
Leaves this humble poet happy
With sleeping dogs and rainy weather.

Kareem Abdul-Jabbarwocky

'Twas thrilling when the Boston Celts
Did L. A. Lakers meet in Boston.
All rabid were the sportsfans,
But the Celt coach spoke with caution:

"Beware the Jabbar hook, my Celts!
The short hook left, the sky hook right!
Beware the fall-away, and stop
The fast-breaking magic act!"

The Celtics took the game in hand;
Long time the fearsome D they played—
So rested they at halftime,
And plotted strategy.

And, as the second half began,
The Larry Bird, with hair of flame,
Came flying past the midcourt line,
And dribbled as he came.

One, two! One, two! And through and through,
The nets of twine went snicker snack!
The Celtics built a big lead;
Then they lost it back.

And hast thou slain the Jabbar hook?
Accept awards my beamish Bird.
A ring, a check, a sportscar,
Are yours, and well deserved.

'Twas thrilling when the Boston Celts
Did L. A. Lakers meet in Boston.
All rabid were the sportsfans.
"Beat L. A.!" was heard often.

The Goldfinches
for Mary Korte

take a walk with me up the lane
             in the evening quiet

parnum paving freds and barneys
         done for the day we walk

little yellow birds!
the little yellow birds are out
our good little bug eating buddies
more numerous than the swallows now
they flit and fly
these compact mirth making avians

the only good thing about star thistle—
the little yellow birds like it

we walk, we stroll, we meander
the little yellow birds meander too

they're not solemn
they're not worried
they're not constantly
engaged in internal dialogue

hail to thee, little yellow!
birds you certainly are

beautiful
     little
          yellow
               birds
       beyond words

The Pull

i wish i could remember
all the things i remember
wish i knew all the things i know

sometimes at night when the light is right
when the moon is just past full
i can feel the pull

    on earth these days
    there are so many people
    it gets complicated
    it's hard to hear

        at night though at night
        things quiet down and
        if you listen you're
        likely to hear

        you're likely to start
        picking up signals
        on a clear channel

moonlight
and maybe a little whiskey
maybe you're drinking bourbon and ginger ale
maybe it's a night in early june

a picture forms itself in your mind's eye
perhaps extraterrestrial intelligence is involved

    forget all the things
    you are supposed to know
    forsake all your schooling

    listen for rhythms

chants and songs

snails creep slowly toward target corn
thousands of children sleep

     we sleep we all dream
     only some of us
     remember

close your eyes
look inside
shut your mouth
listen

     corn, beans, squash
     peppers, tomatoes, potatoes

divine
    intelligence
       that irradiates
          the cosmos
except for certain parts of new jersey

quiet quiet quiet
listen
there *are* magic words
that's what you're listening for

     keep a pen and
     notebook by your bed
     maybe the magic words
     will come to you
     in a dream

       be ready
       keep yourself in shape

it's a moonlit night in early june
in northern california
this night and all nights that have ever happened
are part of the magic

the words and the magic and the night
are all the same thing

it's a gift
don't forget to say
thank you

The Golden Lights of Conviviality
for Wendell Berry

When we came home from drinking
That night in Missoula, Mark was
"Tryna call Terri in Micronesia"
He "couldn' get 'er" he crashed
Abbott and Jackie were so nice
Mary was a honeybunny of course
Glenn told stories chewing coca leaves
20,000 feet in the Andes
Archaeologists abounded
We had killed two chickens for dinner

Sharon Doubiago and the W. L. A.

in memory of Tillie Olsen

I met Sharon Doubiago at the Western Literature
Association annual conference last fall in Sacramento.
Cutting through the restaurant and bar by the
Reflecting pool of the swank Raddison Hotel—
There she was, sitting at a table writing, rapt.
I later learned she was working on an essay about
Her father and boyfriends and Jack Kerouac.
What was it, Sharon? Hobo Jack, Hobo Sunset,
Hobo *something.* You see I attended the session,
"Kerouacian Themes in the Work of Sharon Doubiago."
Three academics presented learned papers about *Hard
Country* with reference to *On the Road.* They were
Very kind to Sharon, less so to old dead Jack.
But never mind. What's an academic hack supposed
To know about spontaneous prose, or the magic land
At the end of the road, or real hard country
For that matter. But they have their place. And
The respondent, Ms. Doubiago, graciously accepted
Their praise and read her nascent essay on Kerouac.

I attended another session where Sharon read poetry.
Now that was pretty good. Two or three other poets
Read too, including my man Gerald Locklin.
I like that—hearing differences in voice, subject
Matter and approach. Tillie Olsen was in attendance at
That one. She's a big fan of Sharon's work. Earlier there
Had been a plenary session with four other poets including

Jane Hirshfield and Beth Lisick, a young punk poet girl from
Berkeley. After Sharon's reading I talked with Tillie.
She was a bit testy, told me: "Sharon should have read
At that plenary session. *She's* a *real* poet, unlike that
Bitter young girl." (Meaning Lisick.) "Well, she's taking

A punk rock stance," I attempted to appease, to no avail.
Tillie: "Oh, a child of wealth, and all that anger!"

I talked with Sharon later. She didn't seem to care
About plenary sessions or concurrent sessions. She
Just seemed happy to be back in California. Sharon
Told me I remind her of her brother, which sounds
Good to me. We need all the brothers and sisters
we can get, for mutual strength and support
In the ongoing quest for peace, love and poetry
In this strange new world of these laughable latter days
Of this so-called American Century.

This year the W. L. A. conference will be in Oklahoma City.
But I think I'll stay home, work on a long pome,
Maybe one of these years they'll have a session about me.

JK's Cats

jack kerouac's cats in heaven,
mewing and mewling.
he feeds them often.
they come around purring to be held.
jack picks up his kitties,
noticing but not interrupting
serious and joyful conversations
with goethe, spengler, proust, nietzsche,
hermann hesse, babe ruth and dizzy dean.
groucho marx and w. c. fields stop by.
neal is in the next room with women.
count basie is leading the orchestra,
consists of buddy bolden,
lester young, charlie parker,
louis armstrong and many others.
jerry garcia on electric guitar.
angel harpo on harp.
kerouac pets his kitty tyke.
his kitty davey rubs his leg.
his mother is beaming but
has finally let him go.
tyke purrs, jack chuckles
and laughs .
he's talking to thomas wolfe
about the american west.
geronimo nods in corroboration.
more cats purr.
angel bartenders pour more beer.
free beer!
another lovely day for kerouac
and his cats in heaven.
they got no complaints.

Three Cats

Six A.M.
Three cats
Come inside
Have a bite
Drink water
Lick themselves
Lie down
Go to sleep—
Good morning!

Purr

"Life is what happens to you while
you're busy making other plans."
                    —John Lennon

kitty cat purr lap
purr lap kitty
cat is cat
furry cat
furry purry
cat kitty
ditty

tongue lick furry cat
purr fur kitty
tongue lick leg
scratch
furry cat
purry cat
sit lap
take nap
little cat
tail flap
nap

Afternoon With Chickens
Kihei, Maui

chickens cluck and strut
    chickens are
        skittish critters

the little worn-out looking
    white duck
     named Hurdy Gurdy
   sits on her eggs
       it's been
       30 days now
  and still no ducklings

Guy Buffet's Pigs of Pukalani
grace our bedroom wall now
it's the day after Winter Solstice

Tim and I
  went to the Sufi dancing
 in Puunene last night
    tonight
  a bunch of folks
 up in Kula
  are going caroling

I got shrimp quiche
    and salad
   at Kihei Natural Foods
    for 3.25
  for lunch today
  came home and
   started reading
   Open Eye, Open Heart
    by Lawrence Ferlinghetti

which inspired me

I took off walking
and ended up
at Charley Young Beach
where I ogled and
went for a swim

then I walked back home
picking up a six pack
of San Miguel beer
for 3.29 at Foodland
on the way

now I'm on the front porch
the afternoon front porch
and the chickens
have disappeared

After Ferlinghetti

I think I'll do it too

sing another mad song

in the human zoo

why not

sit on the front porch

pen and notebook ready

sing another mad song

for freedom

For the Dark-Haired Dark-Eyed Waitress
Who Serves Larry Ferlinghetti His Spaghetti

I met an angry poet on the street,

North Beach, San Francisco.

He had just stolen

a book of poems

by Lawrence Ferlinghetti

from City Lights Bookstore—

"Yeah," he growled,

"I like to see what the big shots are up to."

Ferlinghettinfluences

Joyce, Prevert, Apollinaire

he went to France
and studied their
egalitarian atmosphere

Williams, Cummings, Yeats

in open air
neath reeling sky
goat-footed balloon
and horsemen passed by

Miller, Sandberg, Wolfe

looked homeward to
Nathan's hot dogs
modern times
America's western shore

leaving the City of Lights
to found City Lights
there to lead a quiet life
every day

except on rare occasions
like trials, protests, trips to prison
(where no jailed birds sang sang)

or Bixby Creek
to start all over
reading Whitman
cover to cover

and which of us
has known his mentor

NC

I remember, yes, I recall
skipping rocks, playing football
I recall, yes, I remember
Denver streets in gray November

down Curtis Street
down Larimer
dodging trucks running

I remember, yes, yes
      walking with Father
          by the Platte
               River in winter
                    and spring
                        summer
    fall

like I say

playing football
pool or pinball

and whiling away whole days
in barbershops
or afternoons in movies

always reading
always dreaming
and of course girls
and of course cars

but that came later

what I'm talking about now
are those early days with Father
those childhood days in Denver

yes, ah, hoom, ah, hoom, ah, yes, yes

Two Kerouac Pomes

(1)

I saw the ghost of Jack Kerouac
at the San Francisco S. P. Depot
walking up the track.
He's come back, I thought,
it hasn't all been told.

(2)

I saw Jack Kerouac
in Heaven in a Vision in a Dream
with his pot-
belly and his
poetry and beer.
John Wayne was with him,
and Babe Ruth,
and Dizzy Dean,
and W. C. Fields.
They were sitting, talking, drinking beer.
They had given up cigarettes.

Too Bad

Summer of '74, just out of college,
My friend Mike Plonowski and I decided
To hitchhike up through New England to Eastern Canada.
We had some good times, and mostly good luck.
We slept on the beach at Marblehead, Massachusetts,
In an open field in New Hampshire,
In a climbers' shelter on Mount Washington.
We hitched on up to Quebec, then West to Montreal.
Our French wasn't great but we got by,
Stayed at Youth Hostels, met lots of people, saw the sights.
In Montreal a big gathering was going on,
L'internationale Festival de Jeunesse Francophone—
The International Festival of French Speaking Youth.
There were concerts, dances, poetry readings.
We wandered wondering
And eventually hitched out of Montreal, the Festival still
In full swing. There were lots of people hitching so
We walked out of town a ways along the highway
Trying to find a good spot to hitch.
As we were doing this two French girls approached us—
Pretty, appealing, long-haired in skirts, boots, peasant
Blouses and denim jackets. One of the girls said something
To us rapidly in French that I didn't catch, and Mike didn't
Either because he said, "I'm sorry, we don't speak French."
"Ah," she said, "Eez too bad for you." And they walked away,
Leaving us wondering what we had missed.

Very Cozy

There was a bar we used to hang out at in Ostende,
A dark, down-the-stairs cellar bistro with good beer.
You could even get bread, cheese, a bowl of soup or noodles.
Lots of young people hung out there, the international crowd.
I knew a couple of friendly Scotsmen, some German guys and girls,
Some Swedes, a Greek, some Dutch, French and Belgians.
We'd talk, play guitars and sing, just hang out.
Wish I could remember the name of the place.
My favorite beer was a Belgian ale, Duvel.
One night I was talking to a nice local girl.
She had some English and I a little French,
So we did okay. Just a nice girl, talking.
And she said something to me I'll always remember,
Really probably the highest compliment I've ever received,
It made me feel so warm and comfortable. It still does.
What she said was, "I think you are a very cozy person."
"Thank you," I said, "I think you are a very cozy person too."

Clochard

Je suis seulement un clochard
Flotant comme un bouchon sur la mer.[*]

This happened in Southern France.
Estagel, I believe it was, or Latour de France.
He was a little, one-armed bum,
Un clochard (avec un chien).
It was early morning in a cafe.
He was knocking back a brandy.
 "Chattanooga Choo-Choo" was on the radio.
 "Pardon me boys, is that the Chattanooga choo-choo?"
 "Yes, yes." Track twenty-nine.
He knocked back the brandy, neat.
He looked at me. He smiled
And shrugged, as if to say,
 "Ah, *mon ami,* we know the world,
But anyway, *Salut!* Here's to another day."

---

*   I am only a hobo
      Floating like a cork on the sea.

59

In Paris

There was a man in Paris
the first day I arrived,
so happy to be in Paris,
to really be in Paris
walking the fabled streets
with my rucksack
high and happy.

The man caught my eye.
He was a Meher Baba kind of guy.
He kept smiling.
We were walking in opposite directions,
but I would look back, smiling,
and he would be looking back, smiling.
Again and again and again it happened—
smiling, always smiling, as if to say:
"Oui, Daniel, you really are in Paris,
and it's okay to be this happy."

In Uddevalla

I walked into the town of Uddevalla
from out at Bertil's flat, half crazy.
I think I really was mildly psychotic that day.
Something was going on in the town square.
The reason I had been drawn there.
Some kind of rally for Nature,
with needy chidren,
and beautiful women.
I was Billy Jack, smoldering
in my t-shirt and jeans.
I could help them.
I wasn't going to let women and children
and trees be mistreated.
No sir, not me.

I can't remember what came of it.
It all turned out okay.
I didn't do anything too outrageous.
Didn't get arrested anyway.
I guess I shouted a little (a lot?),
smiled at the children,
flirted with the women—
made a few friends and enemies.
I calmed down after awhile,
walked back to Bertil's
and helped him drink beer.
But for awhile there I was riding high,
out of the West with a white hat,
a little too high behind the rallying cry,
"Freedom for all sentient beings!"

Hokan and Svencon and Me

On the West Coast of Sweden, hard by the North Sea,
Lies the town of Uddevalla, a place you should see.
It was in Uddevalla on a Thursday afternoon
In early September, just past the full moon,
That Hokan and Svencon and Thomas and I,
and one other guy we knew,
Climbed to the top of the town's highest hill,
and got drunk and enjoyed the view.
When we came down we bought kir and beer,
and played frisbee in the park.
Then we rode the bus to Bertil's flat
and drank some more after dark.
I can't remember what happened next;
It seems to have slipped my mind.
I heard that Svencon fell in the river.
He must have been stone drunk blind.
This story has no moral. It's just a matter of fact.
I left Uddevalla soon after that and I never have been back.
But I'll always remember Hokan and Svencon and Thomas,
and the other guy too,
And that fine afternoon, high on a hill,
we got drunk and enjoyed the view.

Vernal Equinox

druids are dancing
rings around oaks
in old groves
chanting riddles
and spelles of olde

the son arrives
ascends his throne
praised by bird song
bud and flower

earth is ancient
earth is new
druids dance
the circles chant
the olde songs spelles
and riddles of the crewe

Nuages of the New Age

like volcanic islands rising from the sea
like baby geckoes falling from the trees

                the new world emerges

like a vestigial fable written on the wind
like the final fist on Muhammed Ali's chin

                the new truth emerges

more disjointed than Joan Didion
more enigmatic than Gunga Din

                new forms emerge

Johnny Lennon
took his pen and
wrote a little song:

Bobby Dylan
are you willin'
to die for all this killin'?

Margie Mead
are we agreed
human character is almost unbelievably malleable?

Jesus Christ
must we believe
the Pope really is infallible?

Ode to Kikkoman Soy Sauce

Sitting in a bottle
Ready to serve:
Water, wheat, salt,
And soy beans, preserved.
Pour it over noodles,
Pour it over rice.
It's naturally brewed.
It sure smells nice.
"Since 1630,"
The label proclaims,
An "all-purpose seasoning"
For Christian or Jain.
Kikkoman soy sauce!
Enhancer of beans!
Brewed in Walworth, Wisconsin,
Soy sauce of dreams!

Ode to Jay Johnstone

Oh My God!?!?!
What's he doing now???
He's out there in left field
with shaving cream or something,
goofing for the cameras
and flirting with the girls.
If it wasn't for his bat
and his general *joie de vivre*
he wouldn't even be in the lineup.
Look at his record.
Where to begin?
O My God!!!
Where to begin???
With Angel flights,
White Sox scandals,
A's for effort?
Or Philly bloop playoff hits,
Yankee pinstripes,
Padre prayers,
Dodger home runs.
Chicago ivy-true craziness,
left-field, right field,
clubhouse antics.
Returning to the field
after between inning
God knows what.
Batting practice always
a little out of whack.
But somehow managing
to survive
and in fact bop
and swing,
a journeyman joker
with a World Series ring.

Three Hacks

sitting

summertime
sitting around
listening to
a ball game
Reds vs. Padres
on my transistor
radio curve ball
misses high fast
ball misses low

summertime

sitting around listening
to a ball game
Reds vs. Padres on my
transistor radio
curve ball misses high
fast ball misses low

hits and misses

sitting summertime around
to a ball game listening
curve ball Reds versus
fast ball Padres on my
high low transistor radio

October Poem for the Ems

Storms move down from Alaska.
Rains wash Eugene.

Gone are those golden
Summer night beer games.

I dream of some more perfect October
With post-season play on all levels.

Somehow the Emeralds have survived into October.
The rain is still here, but it doesn't matter.

The team is on the field.
"Play ball!" the umpire cries.

The stands are full for a Thursday night game.
Playoff intensity fills the air.

On campus and down on the mall
Nobody cares about football.

In pulp mills, on farms folks call:
"How do ya think the Ems'll do this fall?"

Two Baseball Haiku

Little League season
ping of bats
across the river

afternoon bike ride
last day of baseball season—
going, going, gone

Ode to Carmen Salvino

Oh Carmen! To think you could have settled

for life as a semi-pro in Schenectady.

Instead you grabbed the gold ring!

You took your bags and balls and shoes and

gloves and resin and shirts and socks

and towels and slacks

on the road

to Akron
and Cleveland
and Lima, Ohio

to Milwaukee
and Madison
and Michigan

where you rolled and kegled courageously

against pros from all over.

From Denver to Dover

from Winston-Salem to Seattle

you battled the breaks

and the bad boards

and the 3-5-7 split.

You never quit, Carmen—

you came out kegling

and always gave it your best shot

whether you finished in the money or not.

Ode to Bob Hayes

They say Neal Cassady
    was the fastestmanalive.
But I once saw Bob Hayes run a 60-yard dash
    indoors on boards.
If Neal was really faster than that
    he must have been something indeed.
Bullet Bob exploded out of the blocks,
    I mean EXPLODED.
It was over before there was time to think.
Bang! Six runners off and away—
    Bullet Bob the class of the field.
The noise! The speed! The excitement!
Whoosh! Whoah!?! How was he going to stop?
He was going to run through a wall!
Lookout! He did it!
He ran so fast he dematerialized
    and ran right through a wall!
Don't be silly.
There was a ramp going out of the stadium.
He stopped out in the hall
    and came back smiling, waving to the crowd.
Fastest man alive—Bullet Bob Hayes.

Ode to Ed

　　　Yeah, Ed, I knew you when we were kids,
knew you in the old days on Wicklow Road
　　　when we used to play whiffle ball
　　　with the roof in play
　　　　you made up the rules
and Mike and Tim and I
ran laughing and tripped and
putted in the upstairs bedroom.

　　　Yeah, you were a goofy kid
and so was I and weren't we all
back in those Leave It To Beaver days.

　　　And then … what happened?
People who weren't supposed to, died.

　　　　　DIED DEAD

　　and never coming back again

　　　　　buried in the cemetery

　　　　　GONE.

　　　Yeah, heavy sigh.

　　　Did you cry?
　　　I didn't cry for a long time.
I never cried when Mother died,
I died inside.

　　　　What happened next?
　　We went away to college.
　　We looked for clues.
　　The '60s were just ending,

73

Turbulent decade of change.
What did we know?
Kids from Louisville,
What did we know about the great forces

Shaking the decade, shaping our lives?
Just trying to get a clue.
Victims of the sixties?!?!?
You and me both, brother.
What did it mean?
What was the synthesis we began to comprehend
when we first heard the Beatles crooning tunes
our parents never dreamed of,
and heard Simon and Garfunkle harmonizing?
And then along came Mary.
The winds of change were blowing our minds.
Like the man says—

I've tripped and I can't get down.

So we started reading.
Yeah, we read Hesse and Heinlein, Sartre, Camus,
Kierkegaard, Nietzsche. And Snyder, Ferlinghetti, Corso,
Ginsberg, Burroughs. And Heller, Vonnegut, Kerouac, Kesey.

Then I packed my backpack and hit the road.
Rucksack Revolution here I come!
Let me at those roads!

"Oh the times
they are
a-changing."

For Paula, Her 27th Year

When you were born
I came home from school,
Karen said: Mother brought
home the new baby. I
looked at you, so little,
with wrinkled fingers, wee
toes, little baby baby-blue
eyes and fell in love.

Hard to believe now really,
27 years later, lots of so
much bridge over the water,
lots of karma between then
and now, eh? You in Nash-
ville, me and Mar and Nate
in Chico. I can still remember,
all these years and miles,
you're that baby blue-
eyed girl I'll always love.

Mr. Gandhi

Reporter: "Mr. Gandhi, what do you think of Western civilization?"
Mr. Gandhi: "I think it would be a good idea."

The stuffed shirts of England choke on their roast beef
    at the sound of his name

The good people of India take hope
    at the thought of his persistence

The violent tremble in impotent rage
    at his pacifism

He spins the straw of empire
    into the gold of independence

His peace is practiced
    rather than preached

May his ways and days be remembered
    in all times and places

May the example of his courage
    give us strength to carry on

When you think of him
    be calm

Live lives of peace and kindness
    in his name

Feel Like a Poem

Afternoon after
teaching boys about pre-
fixes and suffixes at the
Buddhist Boyhs Scoohl
I'm back home in the
sunny backyard with
leaves. Ah, yes, there
are things I could do
but I sit and scribble.
I feel like a poem. Yes.
A big poem of little pine
trees and tall oaks. A
poem of garden sheds
and cellars. A poem of
ripe fruit and pumpkin
time. Rabbits in their hutches.
Cats in the kitchen waiting
to be fed. And the sun
through the trees, the play
of leaf shadows on a
path. Wood piled waiting
for winter. Gutters cleared
yesterday, debris still
litters the ground around
the house. (One of the things
I could do.) Dishes in
the sink. (Another.)
Good reviews, bad
reviews, stories and
plays waiting to be
written. Books to read
and write. I don't care.
I'm here now in my
shorts with sunshine—
that's enough. Old Bull

Burroughs, Old Bull
Balloon, Someone's in the
Kitchen with Dinah, I
don't care. All my

life too lazy I don't care.
You can come see me
you can be lazy you can
feel like a poem too.
Why not? Autumn
afternoon the lawn chairs
are arranged for
imaginary passengers on
a make believe airline.

Qualified overqualified
underqualified I continue
to write. Sitting in
the sun honey. You can't
do this for money.
Trees. Like trees.
I'm hanging with trees.
We seldom argue, we
mostly agree. Birds
too. I been hearing
some new birds lately.
I like to hear them in
the morning. Unidentified
unexplained I don't care.
Maybe they're travelling
maybe they just got home.

I may go do some
of those things now I
think a good case could
be made now for doing

something else, something
more, shall we say….
productive—something
that contributes to and
promotes the health and
well-being of the family,
the household, the community.
Of course musing, of course
poetry, does that too.

And don't you forget it.

Farm

"We cannot keep things from falling apart in our society
if they do not cohere in our minds and in our lives."
—Wendell Berry

The farm is a finite form.
It has boundaries and gophers,
Obsidian and frogs.
It has an old Volkswagen van
And an apple orchard.

In spite of its limits the farm
Is complex rather than simple.
It involves careful attention,
Constant and ongoing attention,
Playful and serious attention,
To the mysteries of husbandry.

In rainy weather and sunshine,
Through flood years and drought,
The farm and its animals and
Water, trees, soil, air, grasses
Continue to learn and grow.

It takes a lifetime.
It can take many lifetimes.
It's certainly not just for us.
It's for our children's children's children,
And their children.
It really is.

It's for personal health
And the health of the planet.
It's for cities as well as the country.
It may not be the only dance there is,
But it's a damned good one to learn.

The Old Horseplayer
for Paul Wight

"All of life is six-to-five against."
                    —Damon Runyon

He doesn't go to the track much anymore.
He's 87 years old for Christ's sake.
Yeah, they've got elevators now,
and those little golf carts
that'll pick you up at your car.
But that means extra tips,
and then there's the drive, the cost of gas.
With off track betting and cable tv,
There's really no need to go to the track.
And anyway, as he likes to say,
"They wouldn't have those places if people won."

Still he buys his *Racing Form* every day—
his son drives him to the corner store—
and he places a few bets.
What the hell? They're still running.
There are some good young jockeys at Churchill Downs.
He still knows a few trainers.
Why not risk a few dollars?

The old horseplayer spends a lot of time with his son.
His son is 55 now. He drives the old man around.
He and his sisters took away the old man's car keys a few years ago.
He called a locksmith and had a new set made.
They took those away too.
So now he's resigned himself and his son drives him.
They drive out River Road.
"That's where the Pine Room used to be,"
he tells his son. "I remember the night it burned down."
They drive out U. S. 42, past some of the horse farms.

There's still something about a yearling
that makes his heart leap up.

Back home he calls a friend at OTB,
bets $10 on a horse
he likes in the 3rd at Saratoga.
"Never bet on anything that can talk,"
he tells his son.
"Okay Dad, I won't."
"If it rains, go to the movies."
"Thanks for the advice."

Yeah, the old horseplayer has seen a lot.
His wife died a year ago.
He's been lonely since then,
but he's hanging in there.
He's got his kids and grandkids,
and church, and the horses.
He's making a novena at St. Leonard's,
praying he'll live to 105.
Why not? The odds are long,
but they are still posted.
Why not stick around, see what happens next?
Maybe there will be another great horse,
like Sir Barton, or Man O' War, or Secretariat.
Maybe there will finally be another Triple Crown winner.

He walks to the kitchen, pours an iced-tea.
His son comes in the back door.
"Drive me to the corner, will ya?
I need to buy the *Racing Form.*"

Guidelines for the Marathon

for Robin Rule and Daniel Essman,
organizers of many marathon poetry readings
to benefit public libraries in Willits, California

Guidelines for the marathon
poetry reading
5 minutes
5 minutes
5 minutes
in a round
Robin? 5
minutes in a round
robin format,
right, Dan?

In Willits
at Burning
Rock.
In Willits
at Burning
Burning
burning for the ancient heavenly connection
to the starry dynamo in the machinery
of Saturday night
in America
as the sun goes down
stumbling
to the heart
of Saturday night
in Willits
California
Amurka.
5 minutes
in a round
format, Robin?
Among the Dans

at Burning Rock
Gallery on Commercial.
Is that right?
On Commercial
Street or Road
or Avenue?
Or left at
5 P. M.?

5 P. M. to Midnight?
Hell, why not make it
5 A. M. to
Midnight?
It's a marathon
it's poetry
it's useful
it's necessary
it's a benefit
it's fun
it's far out
it's a good cause
it's for the fookin' library
for books
like Henry Miller
says, I look
forward to a time
when work will be forgotten
and books assume
their rightful
place in life.
So, yes
yes yes my
mountain flower
yes i said yes
why not make it
5 A. M. to Midnight

and then put on
another shift
Midnight to 5 A. M.
workin' the
graveyard shift
outa Willits
poetry division
Shakespeare Squad
at the marathon
at the marathon
at the marathon
poetry reading
in a round form
at Robin.

And you know
that first mile
of poetry
is easy
it's those last
25 miles
385 yards
of poetry
that'll test you.

—*ainsi soit il*

Walking Away from
Los Angeles International Airport

I thought I could do it.
I wasn't sure I could do it.
I had a bet with myself I could do it.
Walk away.
Just walk away
From Terminal A, Terminal B,
The International Terminal—
Take off walking
In a direction opposite to the direction of traffic,
Go against the flow and walk away.

I picked up my one carry-on bag,
Exited the building and kept going.
I followed an airline-employee-looking man
Across a lane of airport-entering traffic,
Out past parking lots away—
Away from the airport to Sepulveda Boulevard.

To Sepulveda Boulevard to breathe the free air
Of Sunday afternoon nothing to do get in the car
And see where you end up Los Angeles.
I walked up past airport motels, more airport parking—
Big 747's still noisy overhead coming in for landings—
Past corner bar, adult books and videos, beer and pastrami,
Big screen football, past produce and drugs to
Quintessential Sunday afternoon Sepulveda Boulevard
In & Out Burger—
Most happening place in the neighborhood.
I'll have a burger, fries, a coke—why not?
This must be America.

And kept walking.

Took a left and kept walking
Away from connecting flight,
Adult responsibilities,
Monday morning workaday world.
The workaday world sucks! I walked
Away from wife, children, tv, phone, car, mortgage
Walked, walked—like Jesus, walked—like Kerouac said,
"The world should be built for footwalkers," walked
West in the direction of continent's end walked west

Into the sunset walked
West to the golden shore where Whitman once gazed
West to the Pacific Ocean.

I don't know how I did it.
I was in a trance, in a dream,
In a Sunday afternoon L. A. haze
I guess but it happened. Before I knew it
My feet were wet, I was speechless,
Salt-sprayed, vast, empty, awake,
And I gave up, I surrendered, I was
Pharblongent, I didn't care and I
Wasn't walking anymore I was laughing.

I was peaceful, serene even.

I found it in me at that time,
Standing there wet on an ordinary Sunday afternoon
In the Pacific Ocean, having successfully walked away
From Los Angeles International Airport,
To forgive America,
To forgive the goddamn good old U. S. A.
All her extravagances, presumptuousness,
Military industrial manifest destiny
My country right or wrong
Flag-waving jingoistic bullshit

And just exist and breathe,
Systole and diastole, ebb and flow,
Swell and groovy.

I didn't care anymore.
I had given up.
I was no longer a part of it,
Whatever it was—
No more a part of it than
That seagull, that kelp strand.

And there I vanished.
No way back to the airport.
No return flight.
No more me.
No more modern world.
The age of autogeddon
Had come to an end.

Words at One A.M.

Tonight up reading Rimbaud and Baudelaire,
beautiful poetry and prose. Prose poetry.
The beautiful drunken moon. The belief that it can all be
written out, expressed, at least attempted, with words.
An amazing game. An amazing conceit. A ridiculous ambition.
A possibility. To turn words into shining symbols. To invest
them with such shining reflecting attraction that they are
irresistible and move and shimmer like miraculous leaves
in a nourishing breeze. Can it be done? Have Rimbaud and
Baudelaire achieved it at times? They have.
Can I even dream of achieving anything similar?
I can dream.

Prayer

I pray for everyone.
I pray for everyone.
I pray for everyone.
And I pray to become
a better person.
More patient.
More kind.
More helpful.
And a better listener.

978-0-595-49652-5
0-595-49652-0

Printed in the United States
138195LV00002B/2/P

9 780595 496525